Birds

Written by Jilly MacLeod

Contents

Collins

Birds all around

You can see birds all around you.
Look for them flying around in parks and
gardens and at the beach.

Not all birds can fly. The ostrich cannot fly but it can run very fast. The ostrich is the biggest bird of all. It is taller than a man.

Sea birds

Flocks of seagulls swoop in the air by the sea. Seagulls have a loud screeching call. They eat things like fish, crabs and prawns.

You can see puffins on cliffs by the coast. They dive down to grab fish from the sea. Puffins have red and blue beaks. They look a bit like clowns.

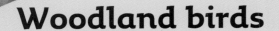

Woodland birds

Woodpeckers tap their beaks on tree trunks and make a loud rat-a-tat sound.
They are looking for insects to eat.

Crows are very clever birds. They can open snails by dropping them on to stones. You can see crows in woods and in towns.

Hunting birds

Owls hunt at night. They can see in the dark and have strong beaks and sharp claws. Owls do not make a sound when they fly.

Hawks hunt in the daytime. They glide high in the air. Then they swoop down to catch small animals on the ground.

Bright birds

Parrots are very bright birds. Some are red, yellow, blue or green. Parrots are often kept as pets. You can teach them to talk.

Peacocks are bright blue and green.
They can make a huge fan with their tails.
People sometimes keep peacocks in their gardens.

Tall birds

Storks are very tall. They have long legs and long slim beaks. Storks love to stand on one leg. They clap their beaks to make a loud sound.

The heron is tall too. It has a very long neck and a strong beak. Herons wade in ponds and streams, looking for fish to eat.

14

Hunting birds

Tall birds

Bright birds

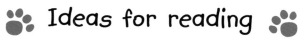

Ideas for reading

Written by Linda Pagett B.Ed (hons), M.Ed
Lecturer and Educational Consultant

Reading objectives:
- apply phonic knowledge and skills as the route to decode words
- listen to and discuss a wide range of non-fiction
- predict what might happen on the basis of what has been read so far
- explain clearly their understanding of what is read to them

Spoken language objectives:
- give well-structured descriptions, explanations and narratives for different purposes
- use spoken language to develop understanding through speculating, imagining and exploring ideas
- use relevant strategies to build their vocabulary
- maintain attention and participate actively in collaborative conversations, staying on topic and initiating and responding to comments

Curriculum links: Science; Variation

Focus phonemes: ow (clown, towns, down), air (air) ir (birds), al (all, taller, small, talk, tall), aw (prawns, claws)

Fast words: you, the, have, they, by, to, very, are, when, some, their, one

Word count: 319

Build a context for reading

- Write the words that feature the focus phonemes *ow* and *air* on a small whiteboard and ask the group to fast-read them, blending aloud if they need to.
- Write three irregular fast words on the whiteboard, e.g. *have, when, their* and ask the children to fast-read them
- Look at the front cover together. Do the children think this is a fiction or non-fiction book? Ask children to give reasons.
- Invite them to read the title together. What might this book tell them?

Understand and apply reading strategies

- Give each child a copy of the book and ask them to read it independently.
- Move around the group listening to each child as they read. If any children are experiencing difficulties, remind them to sound through each phoneme in the word in the order in which it appears.
- Ask fast-finishers to choose their favourite bird. Ask them to think of reasons for their choices to tell the others at the end of the session.
- As you move round, check that children understand some of the more complex words and phrases, e.g. *loud screeching call, rat-a-tat sound.*